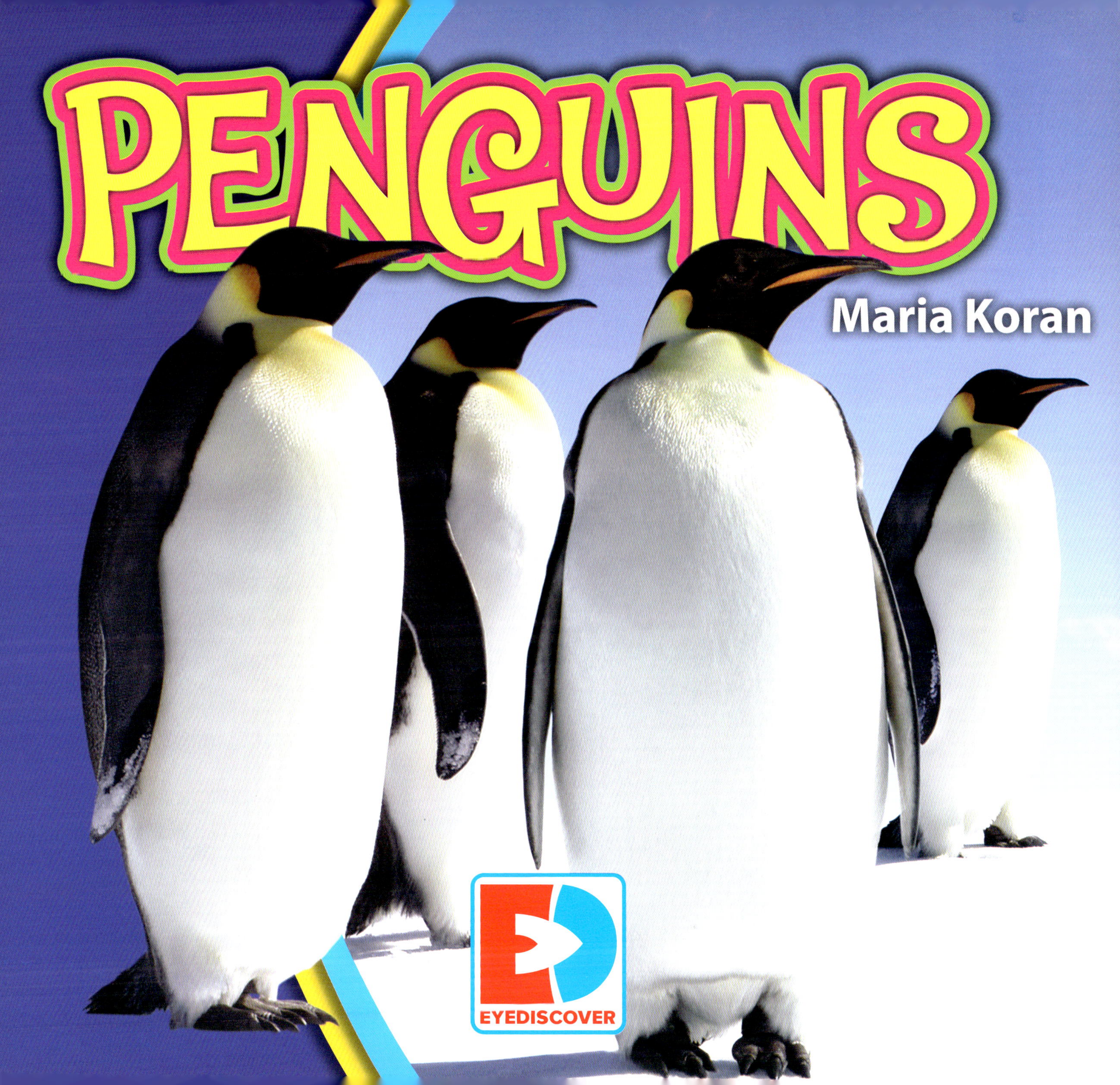
PENGUINS
Maria Koran
EYEDISCOVER

Go to **www.eyediscover.com** and enter this book's unique code.

BOOK CODE

AVQ67422

EYEDISCOVER brings you optic readalongs that support active learning.

Published by AV[2] by Weigl
350 5th Avenue, 59th Floor New York, NY 10118
Website: www.eyediscover.com

Library of Congress Cataloging-in-Publication Data available on request

ISBN 978-1-7911-0750-5 (hardcover)

Printed in Guangzhou, China
1 2 3 4 5 6 7 8 9 0 23 22 21 20 19

072019
121818

Project Coordinator: John Willis
Designer: Mandy Christiansen and Ana María Vidal

Weigl acknowledges iStock, Minden, and Getty Images as the primary image suppliers for this title.

EYEDISCOVER provides enriched content, optimized for tablet use, that supplements and complements this book. EYEDISCOVER books strive to create inspired learning and engage young minds in a total learning experience.

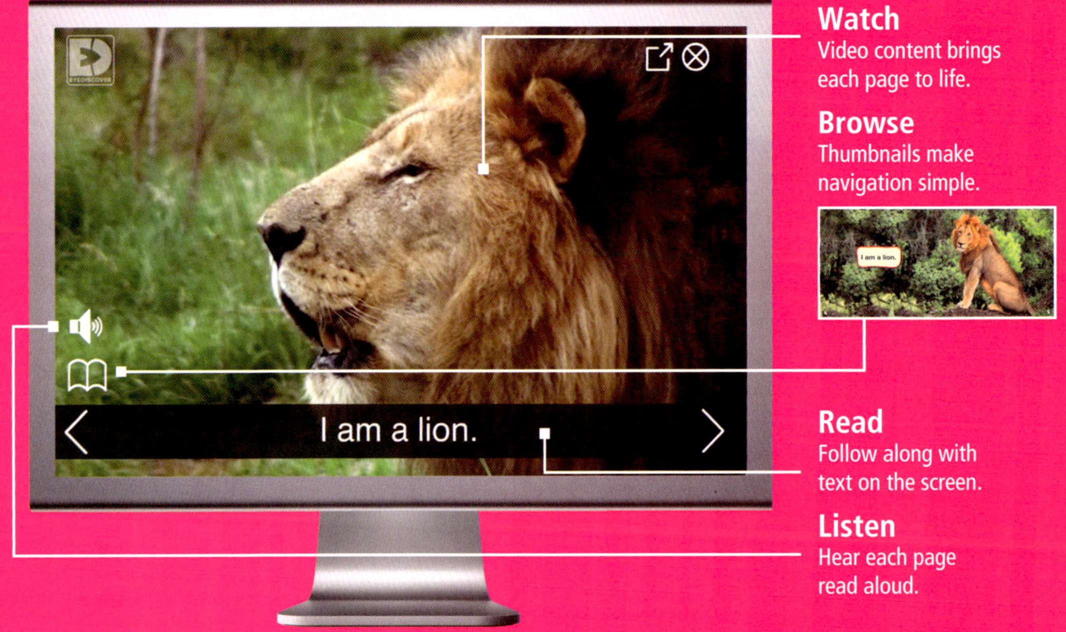

Watch
Video content brings each page to life.

Browse
Thumbnails make navigation simple.

Read
Follow along with text on the screen.

Listen
Hear each page read aloud.

Your EYEDISCOVER Optic Readalongs come alive with...

Audio
Listen to the entire book read aloud.

Video
High resolution videos turn each spread into an optic readalong.

OPTIMIZED FOR

- TABLETS
- WHITEBOARDS

- COMPUTERS
- AND MUCH MORE!

PENGUINS

In this book, you will learn about

- what they are
- how they look
- what they do

and much more!

Penguins are birds that cannot fly. They have black and white feathers.

Most penguins live in very cold places. Their feathers and fat keep them warm.

Penguins swim by flapping their flippers.

Some penguins slide across snow and ice on their bellies. This helps them move faster.

Penguins dive into the ocean to hunt small animals. Penguins can drink salty ocean water.

Penguins do not taste their food. They swallow it whole.

The emperor penguin is the tallest penguin. Fairy penguins are the shortest.

Penguins live in large groups with their chicks. Penguin chicks have very fluffy feathers.

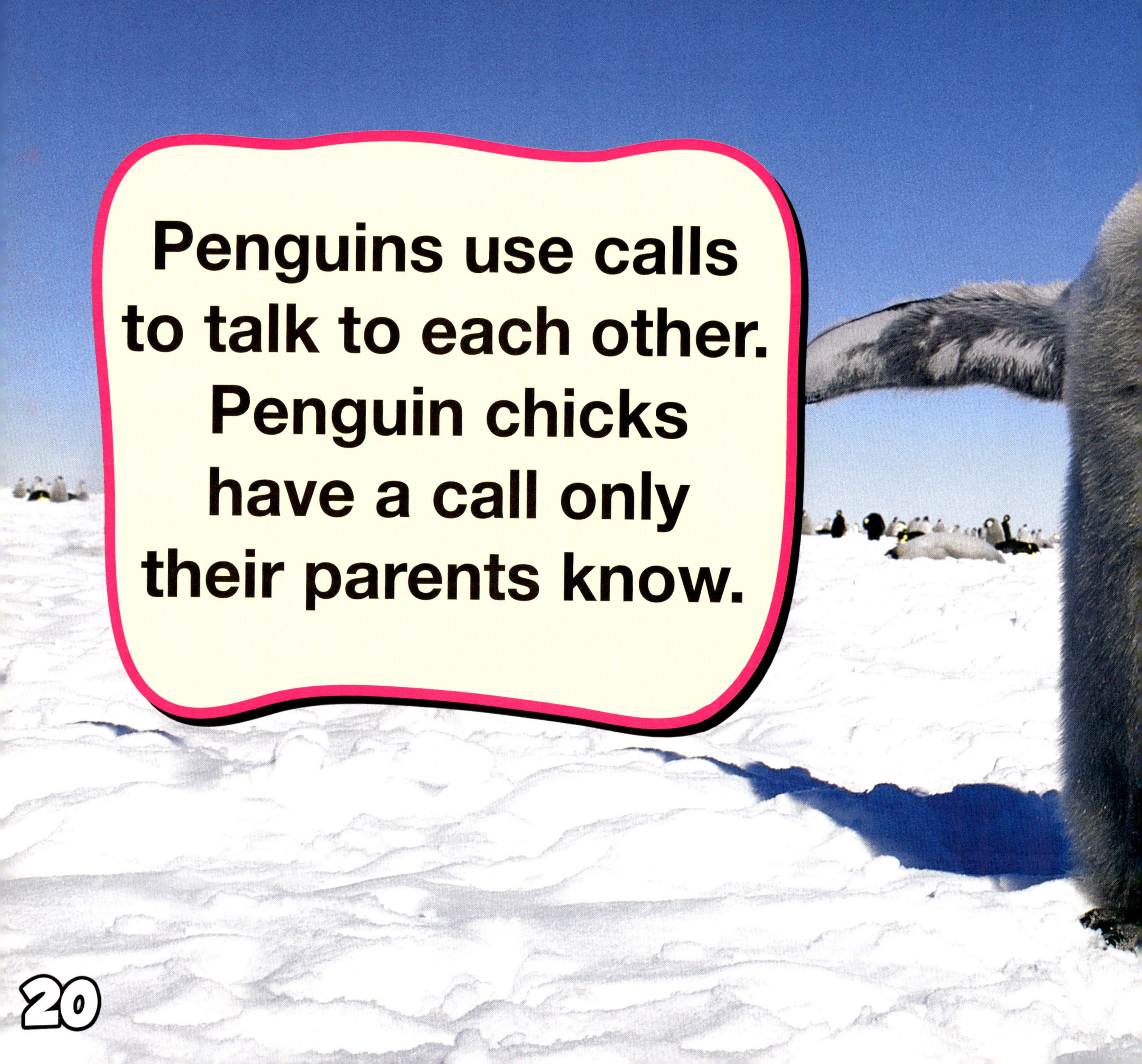

Penguins use calls to talk to each other. Penguin chicks have a call only their parents know.

PENGUINS BY THE NUMBERS

A **fairy penguin** weighs about **2 pounds.** (0.9 kilograms)

An **emperor penguin** is about 4 **feet tall.** (1.2 meters)

There are **18 different** types of **penguins.**

Penguins **live** for about **15** to **20** years.

Penguins have a **third eyelid** that keeps their eyes **safe** underwater.

Penguins usually stay **underwater** for **less** than **1 minute.**

KEY WORDS

Research has shown that as much as 65 percent of all written material published in English is made up of 300 words. These 300 words cannot be taught using pictures or learned by sounding them out. They must be recognized by sight. This book contains 42 common sight words to help young readers improve their reading fluency and comprehension. This book also teaches young readers several important content words, such as proper nouns. These words are paired with pictures to aid in learning and improve understanding.

Page	Sight Words First Appearance
4	and, are, have, that, they, white
7	in, keep, live, most, places, their, them, very
8	by
10	helps, move, on, some, this
12	animals, can, into, small, the, to, water
15	do, food, it, not
16	is
19	groups, large, with
20	a, calls, each, know, only, other, talk, use

Page	Content Words First Appearance
4	birds, feathers, penguins, birds
7	fat
8	flippers
10	bellies, ice, snow
12	ocean
16	emperor penguin, fairy penguins
19	chicks
20	parents

Watch
Video content brings each page to life.

Browse
Thumbnails make navigation simple.

Read
Follow along with text on the screen.

Listen
Hear each page read aloud.

Go to www.eyediscover.com and enter this book's unique code.

BOOK CODE

AVQ67422